For Nicole

Published 1987
by Merehurst Press
5, Great James Street
London WC1N 3DA
by arrangement with
Temps de Pose Editions
12, rue de Sévigné
75004 PARIS
TELEX 215313 F

© 1987 Editions Temps de Pose
Photographs copyright © 1987 : Pierre TOUTAIN
Text   copyright © 1987 : Philippe GANIER RAYMOND
ISBN 0-948075-70-8

Layout : Corinne REYMOND
Photocomposition : Graphelec, Paris and Scheuble & Baumgartner, Berlin
Printed in Italy by SAGDOS-Brugherio-Milano
Translated by Veronica HAMMOND

PARIS

Photographs
Pierre TOUTAIN

Text
Philippe GANIER RAYMOND

MEREHURST PRESS
LONDON

The hostelry of death

In 1793 the Conciergerie, tireless purveyor to the scaffold,
was crammed with prisoners who were under sentence of death within the hour.
(A. Dumas)

Lovers of the Seine

I love beautiful serene evenings, I love evenings...
(V. Hugo)

The fortress of art

Sometimes in the Louvre he would stop in front of old paintings ; and, his love pursuing her into the recesses of time, would substitute her for the ladies in the paintings.
(G. Flaubert)

Paris

I grew up in the area of Paris known as the left Bank. My school was in the rue de Poissy, the swimming-pool was in the rue de Pontoise, outdoor games were in the Arènes de Lutèce; I daydreamed along the Seine. My friends lived in the rue de Bièvre, the last vestige of the medieval Square of Miracles, cut at right angles by the rue Frédéric Sauton. My life was centred around Maubert Square.

In those days in the nineteen forties, a stone pedestal stood in the Square, its green bronze tears still lamenting the vanished statue (melted down by the German occupier to make cannon-bores) of the humanist Etienne Dolet, burned at the stake on that same spot one morning in 1546. Even after death fire clung to Dolet, that companion of liberty who had had the gallant foolhardiness to publish Rabelais' works two centuries before the Age of Enlightment.

It is quite true that my Paris is redolent of gunpowder. I still feel more affinities with a Parisian street urchin such as Gavroche from the pages of *Les Misérables*, yes even now, than with Maurice Chevalier; I am closer to Bruand the poet, Piaf the singer and Marcel Aymé, the most prominent resident of Junot Avenue at Montmartre than to the architects of La Défense, a purpose-built, skyscraper-filled suburb. I did not fall in love with Paris at first sight, but when I succumbed to her charms it was for her outbursts of violence in the sun's heat, for her often intimate celebrations of liberty. Paris is a magnet for artists and intellectuals from all over the world. At first that surprised me, because Paris is a harsh judge and access to its circles is closed to outsiders. For example a famous American writer had to wait patiently for Mr. Caze, the owner of the Brasserie Lipp, to place him at a table on the ground floor. He spent months and months in purgatory on the first floor before being admitted to the paradise of the literary (although not that of the gourmet) where Sartre sat next to Beckett and François Mitterrand near Marguerite Duras, two tables removed from young Günther Grass busy writing the first draft of *The Tin Drum*.

Once I had acquired a cosmopolitan heart and mind, I at last realized why Pascin, Modigliani, Picasso, Juan Gris, Brancusi, Truman Capote and so many other moths of genius had been attracted to the lights of Paris. Paris is really a magnificent woman, infinitely desirable because she so seldom welcomes you with open arms. For an artist such as Ernest Hemingway to come from Minnesota to Paris reveals a two-fold desire to revel in sensuality and to stand up to ruthless judges who could either launch him into fame and fortune or condemn him to wretchedness. It means refusing the easy way out: it is the battling instinct of conquerors.

Paris never lets you rest. Paris is a remarkably elegant minx glancing lovingly at her loafers. Like the great painter Utrillo staggering down the rue des Saules. His ghastly wife, Lucie Valore, insisted on showing her own pictures at all his exhibitions but also kept him alive by preventing him from drinking himself blind at the Café Rose now called Chez Toutoune. Paris is a city of contrasts. Its evolution results both from mistrust and admiration. A city which has become as indispensable as a café which remains open when all the surrounding ones have closed.

Yet Paris is also a foreign city. Remember that two Americans and a German were elected to the *Convention Nationale* in 1793; that Ionesco is Romanian, that the American Julien Green belongs to the Académie Française, whose members are often far more amusing than is generally believed, that Kanas, the Greek painter, invented a revolutionary piece of equipment in La Coupole café. If I survey my friends I find that they have outlandish names such as Slavicek, Breuer, Sarhmann, Semprun-Maura, Ibañez, Garcia, Mehrar, Antonkin, Garzon, Cohen... A Berliner by adoption, a Frenchman born in Joinville, I have loved Paris

Paris, that boundless city...
(Voltaire)

*It is at night
that it is praiseworthy
to believe in Light.
(E. Rostand)*

ever since I realized that foreigners are far more at home here than anywhere else. Their home lies in the triangle formed by three cafés — Le Flore, Lipp, La Coupole — with the Select to fall back on. In this haven of the French intelligentsia looked after by barmen from Auvergne, fifty-six nations congregate. That is my Paris.

From the Saint Eustache Church to the rue Jacob, from the Furstenberg Square to the rue de l'Abbaye you contemplate some of the most beautiful scenery in the world and come across some of the most impressive statues — Baudelaire and Verlaine, Nerval and Balzac, who lived everywhere in Paris. Gabriel's colonnade is one masterpierce, Doctor Dalzace's house is another, as are the few remaining houses designed by Guimard in what was once the old village of Passy. You cannot walk a hundred yards in Paris without being astonished and overwhelmed by the weight of a history which like that of Rome was built on a churchyard — the Catacombs. Paris to me is water, fire and blood.

Cruelty too. One day Toulouse Lautrec forgot his stick in a café. The waiter ran after him and said, "Master, you forgot your pencil".

But Paris for me, as I said before, means gunpowder. I returned to Maubert Square not long ago. The stone base had disappeared. In spite of the renewal of interest in statues and although Mendès France contemplates Baudelaire in the Luxembourg gardens it has occurred to no-one to restore Dolet. Instead he has been replaced by a dark green fountain without any cup. After fire, water.

In the rue de Poissy the fire station stood in a former convent. It is still here, unmentioned by the guidebooks, although one can climb down into the Catacombs through the chapel. During the dark years of the Second World War, until 1943 exactly, every morning at 10 a.m. the trumpet sounded the *Marseillaise* to announce playtime for the school just opposite. Fire, water and liberty.

To a certain extent, in spite of the bombs, the war seemed quite far away. Such was my Paris up to the day when the first yellow stars of David flowered on violet capes in the playground. The season, a season of heavy rains, of "no dogs, no Jews", notices in parks, swept into the polygon of relative liberty bounded to the north by the wharves on the Seine, to the south by the Ecole Polytechnique to the west by the Boulevard Saint Michel and to the east by the rue du Cardinal Lemoine. In July came the round-up of Jews, the firemen no longer trumpeted the *Marseillaise* and in October, there were fewer pupils in the playground. "They persevere, they are going too far," Paul Eluard wrote, "their world is not ours." It was the time of shame without pity. But what glory for Dolet that the first shots of the Liberation of Paris should have been fired in Maubert Square.

When I heard them, I was swimming in the Seine under the footbridge between the Ile Saint Louis and the Ile de la Cité. One day, General Leclerc's tanks appeared in the rue des Bernardins. The soldiers looked like exhausted train-drivers: they had the glazed shiny eyes and the heavy transparent eyelids of men who have known fear. Some were Spanish Republicans. Remember — the first tank to enter Paris had been baptised *Rosita*. Its crew knew only a smatter-

ing of French. After that one came the tanks called *Teruel Brunete, Guadarrama* and *Guadalajara*. Only one survived the war: the four others were blown up near Strasbourg.

There were North African soldiers too, whom people loved in that far past, aloof behind the sights of their machine-guns, tracking the militia-men cornered on the zinc roofs who emptied their cartridge clips before facing the firing-squad. The North Africans sent short, deliberately wild volleys to make it clear, I presume, that this business was no concern of theirs.

I remember that these liberators were dying of thirst. I can still visualize one marine lifting a cast-iron drain cover in the rue Cochin and gulping at the little spray of water which spurted up fitfully. Then came the Americans — worn-out and suffocated by the dust of the countryside. Two black American soldiers, their helmets in their hands, went into the pancake-shop at 38, Boulevard Saint-Germain; the woman was amazed to see the two Blacks use their napkins to clean the grimy forks she had handed them. After the Liberation, Paris spent years eradicating its painful blemishes.

Fire, water and liberty. Young women offered themselves with impulsive grace to the soldiers, without the slightest immodesty of word or gesture, no plunging necklines to be seen in spite of the heatwave. The heat was indeed unbearable. Beetles gorged with nectar from the Luxembourg Gardens splattered to death on the armoured cars. New delightful smells were added to the profusion of scents. Maubert Square became, for days on end, a sensual odoriferous bouquet making everyone dizzy with its multifarious fragrancies — the all-pervading one was that of pink petrol oozing from jerrycans.

However, one night, *they* came back with their planes. The bombs fell on the wine market where General Leclerc's troops were resting off-duty. We heard the ambulances and the muted cries of the wounded whose lives doctors would try to save at the Necker Hospital. It was a night of horror, unmentioned in the history books, because, in my opinion, the groans of the burned are the most unbearable of human sounds.

The Americans set up their anti-aircraft batteries in the gardens of Notre-Dame Cathedral. We used to steal their short shells and unaware of the danger, we took them to pieces behind our desks. In October it was all over. But on August 24, 1944, the resistance fighter André Balland, aged 18, who had attacked the enemy with hand-grenades in the rue des Batignolles, was told that there was still a handful of Waffen SS covered by a tank at Porte de la Villette who had to be dislodged. Balland lay along the left wing of a 11 CV Citroën car with his machine gun awkwardly jammed against his left shoulder (a Czech machine gun probably). The street was quite wide, hazy in the setting sun and clouded with the chalk-white dust of the recent battle. The tank surged out of a sort of shed with the gun of its turret slanted up to the right as if it were gazing upwards. He lay on the cobbles and started flicking bullets at the steel insect, the turret swivelled with an electric whirr. A shell exploded above Balland sending shrapnel into his leg. Two months went by. Balland was a music lover particularly fond of singing. One evening he went to a concert. It was at the Champs Elysées theatre, a masterpiece created by the architect August Perret who was the first to exploit successfully the potentialities of concrete metalwork and who gave Paris the theatre with the best acoustics. Balland arrived late, tripped up in his plaster cast and fell over noisily. The audience hissed insults. It was on the Right Bank of the Seine, not the Left, and history had rapidly turned the page. The elegant areas, even if the echo of events had reached them, wished to hear no more of these sublime children even if they had been the close friends at the Lycée Carnot of the youngest prisoner shot at Chateaubriant, Guy Môquet.

My friends of the rue de Poissy and I often went roller-skating along the rue Valette and the rue des Ecoles and especially along the rue des Bernardins, that short street which puckers into a bottle-neck before arriving at the Seine. The remaining barricades were being thrown into the river. We had arrived too late to become heroes. To compensate, we invented fabulous biographies for ourselves which we told to Nadine, the daughter of the man who ran a second-hand bookshop, or Arlette, the young prodigy at Miss Morel's piano class, or Nicole or Monique, our successive loves. In Paris, at that period one had to be an adult or cease to be. My friend Ducamus, aged eleven, cherished the dream of joining the Second French Armoured Division: I myself was determined to enlist in Patton's army which was waiting at Porte de Clignancourt for orders to go and be slaughtered at Bastogna. With her admirable tactfulness my mother one evening offered me a bag of marbles (real clay ones not plaster) which forced me, most reluctantly, to postpone my enlistment.

At that time, on the Left Bank, tabby cats roamed everywhere and stray dogs ran along the Boulevard. If I remember rightly, after having hugged the walls for four years we could saunter once again, rediscovering that to meander is the most pleasurable way of getting from one point to another. Only a handful of moralists continued to celebrate the virtues of the straight line: among them, a few scoundrels, some of them with make-up on, who taught grammar, maths and geography at my school: the Lycée Henry IV. They outlawed the right to dream and assassinated imagination with a word or with four hours of detention. Claude Roy in his autobiography *Moi, je* has admirably described secondary schools: the halls of totalitarianism, the antechambers of the army and of the camps. There, the wheat was divided from the chaff and objects of compulsory admiration were dictated to us. Nevertheless as Flaubert said about priests: "some of them were all right". I still hate the others, but I owe them a lot. When I was expelled from that yellow prison over which a superb but out-of-bounds tower loomed, my parents discreetly negotiated my enrolment at the Lycée Charlemagne. That was how I discovered the Right Bank.

I already knew something about it thanks to my father, a famous film-maker who took my mother and me every Sunday to the pictures on the Champs-Elysées. We went by tube from the Maubert Mutualité tube station. Like all the others, it was crowned by four lamps embedded in stone: four breasts of thick cathedral-glass that were left unlit in the broad daylight. In Paris at that time perfect strangers spoke to one another in the street and in the tube. The ticket collectors used to wear caps with white braid. They yawned as they punched tickets, sitting under a 1910 by-law which forbade them to drink any spirits except hydromel with water. They wore out their knees on a low steel door and uttered resigned considerations, often characterized by their solid common-sense. Some of them wrote poems of which several have been published. From time to time, they exchanged a rapid handshake with female employees whose hair was drawn tightly under their caps with two combs. This underground world, cool in summer, warm in winter, wafted saltpetre, tolerance and the peculiar fragrance of budding love.

We changed at Sèvres Babylone, then at Concorde. After the Chambre des Députés station the train put on a little burst of speed; we rattled into a perfectly round steel tube; water from the Seine trickled onto the metal caps. In the centre of the earth and twenty thousand leagues under my dreams, delivered at last from my nightmares of school, I could already imagine my film star idols, above all the entrancing Shelley Winters and Kim Novak, who replaced in my daydreams the trapeze artists at the Winter Circus whose thighs, slivers of flesh and silver, had first made my heart throb. My father is a deprecative critic. As we left the cinema, he passed judgement on *The Evening Visitors* or *The Third Man*: "it's not bad but a bit melodramatic". And he explained why. After the demonstration we made our way home to the Left Bank.

In summer, we regularly took the train from Paris-Bastille to Verneuil l'Etang and alighted at Joinville le Pont, where I was born, to go swimming in the River Marne.

The carriages were double-deckers. Every time I came home I had a cinder in my eye. My mother replied to my moans, "Don't think about it" and dragged me along, after having tried, successfully sometimes, to extract the tiny foreign body with the corner of a handkerchief. At the Bastille, there was the boulevard Bourdon where Bouvard and Pecuchet met during a heatwave. But more especially, under the elevated tube lay the dead waters of the Canal Saint-Martin. Couples strolled alongside, on the grass growing between the cobbles. Fishermen tempted the handful of bleaks with paste bait, ignoring the immodest antics of the stray dogs. Fifty yards away, Victor Hugo's character Gavroche, inside a life-size model elephant made of plaster and stucco, had given food to two kids: "Here! Stuff this in your bellies". The century had plenty of elbow room — Hugo had witnessed and recorded perfectly how the age weaved and swerved around the Bastille column.

And then one day the demagogues, the whizzkids of fast culture, got hold of the Canal Saint-Martin. They accumulated those little nothings that allow *parvenus* to destroy secret gardens. A port was created with a double row of stairs leading from the wharf to a skimpy arch left over from Beaubourg. Proud of their work, the local councillors put up a plaque to commemorate their vandalism. With its two ramps and its imported greenery the Canal Saint-Martin is an artefact of idiocy. Whoever you are, do not trample on my adolescence, do not shatter my dreams!

Someone said to me the other day,
"What do you do with yourself?"
"I am busy ageing", I answered.
"It takes up all one's time."
(P. Leauteaud)

How dare you put
birds in cages !
(V. Hugo)

In the middle years of the nineteenth century, much of Paris was demolished and rebuilt by Baron Haussmann who was then the city's mayor. Haussmann broke up Paris and wrecked its history in a sort of romantic frenzy, while at the same time he was obeying strict orders to open large avenues so that the artillery had room to manœuvre if and when barricades went up. It was tragically successful to such an extent that in 1871 the Army massacred dozens of Commune revolutionaries in the cellars of the Opera then under construction. And it is not by chance that the last shots were fired far from the water, by those men of liberty at Belleville which is an area of Paris that Haussmann had left untouched. Let us come back to the Canal Saint-Martin. Haussmann's plan at least had the merit of being clear. It is not true either that he only built heavily-decorated stone buildings. He also left several masterpieces to posterity — I am thinking of the building that housed the penny bazaar *Au gagne petit* in the Avenue de l'Opéra and of the innumerable passages (passage des Panoramas, passage Choiseul). Haussmann destroyed then built up again, quite the contrary of our insipid architecture which could later tenaciously recreate and remodel Paris like smug surgeons in the green belt.

When I studied at the Lycée Charlemagne the roll of a drum still announced the schoolbreak as in Napoleon's time, but the atmosphere was anything but military except for a sadist who taught history ("Laroche, come and get a slap": Laroche came up and got his slap which sent him hurtling into the blackboard). We felt we were loved, even if it was from a distance. My thanks go to Jean Varloot, my teacher of Classics and French, for having introduced me to Diderot and Beaumarchais and other mysteries of liberty hidden behind his mischievous smile.

My friend Frederic acquainted me with the Place des Vosges. His godmother who lived next door to Victor Hugo's house used to make us eggnog. I was madly in love with his cousin Patricia, beautiful and indomitable and with hair as russet as an Indian summer. Once a year there was a Poet's Fair in the Place des Vosges. (It was there I discovered what an acrostic was.) A little man, Jean-Jacques Brousson, trotted along the gravel paths, forever disparaging Anatole France whose secretary he had been.

Day after happy day went by. Every evening I walked back to the Left Bank, down the rue du Petit Musc which led to a garden with a crumbling tower made with stones from the Bastille castle in the centre. Behind me there was the Collège Massillon, a crammer's where Latin and Greek were presided over by ferocious Inquisitors. Or else I went back home via Saint-Paul tube station, past the extraordinary house 68 rue François Miron, a stone backdrop for *Don Giovanni,* where Mozart once lived, and past Saint-Gervais church, sober as a Calvinist chapel except for an organ which had once belonged to François Couperin.

I nearly always stopped at the Brasserie Alsacienne in the île Saint-Louis to scribble down the first draft of my essays. Women dressed in black listened avidly to stubble-chinned haggard actors proclaiming certainties that subsequent phrases undermined. A lonely tormented adolescent, living a stone's throw away from Philippe de Champaigne's studio and Léon Blum's house, I considered myself frightfully intelligent. I still look back regretfully at that smug pretension. The Lycée Charlemagne encouraged my development with the exception of the acrimonious grey-bearded Head of Studies whom we had nicknamed 'Tin Man'. But he was powerless against the libertarian insolence of Askolovitch, of Mittelman, of Kazatikoff, and others, some of them orphans, for the Lycée Charlemagne is next to the Jewish quarter centred on the rue des Rosiers. At the Lycée Charlemagne, in the grey quadrangle surrounded by the formal seventeenth century setting, I experienced in the middle of Paris a feeling which has never left me: a desire to know others better. At Charlemagne, a boy of 15, I became cosmopolitan and rid myself of contempt, the vilest of human feelings. Fire is love, water is the Seine, tolerance is amazed: the whole generates liberty. I am extremely proud to have exchanged a few words with the philosopher Gaston Bachelard in Paris.

In those days one could not get near the Eiffel Tower: there were fantastic queues at the foot of the north-east pillar. One year I earned the money for my holidays showing tourists around the capital since I could already speak English. It was the first and last time that I, with a mass of American women trailing behind me, climbed up to the top of the headless metal woman, her four legs straddling the capital. I felt nothing. The Seine flowed beneath, a bronze braid sewn onto a grey beret. Never pay attention to what people say about Paris — it must not be seen from above but at the level of the cobblestones. Those cobbles that terrify the bourgeois, that give nightmares to those who govern us: cobbles arranged in semi-circles, in shades of grey and pink, revolutionary sweetmeats that disgust the lily-livered. That was in 1968 when, in spite of Haussmann, and twenty-four years after the liberation of Paris, barricades went up but without a single gun on the insurgents'side. An admirable mayor named Grimaud realized that it was a celebration and ordered the police to sheathe their guns. Only idiots were afraid. They nevertheless had the last word. An asphalt stream was poured over the cobbles.

However Paris triumphs over stupidity. In Passy, Guimard's houses in the rue La Fontaine have been preserved, along with the metro stations he designed. The buildings created by Auguste Perret, the greatest architect of our century, have not been pulled down. Buren the artist has been allowed to set up his truncated, striped columns of different sizes in the Palais Royal courtyard, thus enabling idiots who had come in groups to scoff, to discover that eighteenth century display which they had never really seen, used as they were to the rows of ministry cars parked in its heart. The colonnade was designed by the architect Victor Louis who built that other masterpiece: the Bordeaux theatre.

Familiarity has bred love of Paris. I began to love Paris the day people stopped harping upon the fact that the Place Dauphine was the Seventh Wonder of the World. Instead I discovered, by chance and on foot, the area round the rue d'Aligre: its magnificent old tollhouse, its market full of tramps and its cafés full of anarchists. I learned, because I lived there, that Montmartre should not be epitomized by the Place du Tertre. There is, for example at the corner of the rue Doudeauville a café called Le Papillon (The Butterfly) which has a butterfly sign hanging outside. A good dozen ethnic groups congregate there daily to drink, without a hint of fisticuffs. I used to wonder why Paris, where no-one invites people home; Paris, on its guard, as welcoming as a steel safe, attracted foreigners so compulsively. It took me years to realize that Paris is a teeming, sometimes hostile desert with marvellous café oases that Le are its cafés: the Closeraie des Lilas, the Salvi in the rue Delambre, the Liberté on the Boulevard Quinet, the Bon Tabac on the Boulevard Saint Germain... In each of these establishments, some of which are havens for intelligence, you can admire the measured speech and movement typical of the Auvergne man as he gives you your change.

More than two hundred years after the opening of the Café Procope where the philosophers circulated the ideas that were to inspire the French Revolution, intellectuals still frequent cafés and still write in cafés. It used to be said that an editor's contract was signed at Lipp and that the novel was written at La Coupole. There is still some truth in that. Every one can remember how important the Flore was for the existentialist movement, but the regal profile of Samuel Bekkett could be seen there too. Günther Grass played the washboard every evening in a little jazz band huddled in a cellar. Everyone can remember too that when Hemingway came back to Paris with the American forces in 1944, it was to camp literally at the Coupole. Have things changed? Not really, Montparnasse has simply taken back the painters and writers it had hired out to Saint Germain Des Prés on a twenty-year lease. The Closeraie des Lilas has become once again a place where thinkers are at home. You can meet the new philosophers there and the survivors of the *Nouveau Roman*, Sartro-Hegelians now devoting themselves to ego-centred literature. Philippe Sollers and Jean Edern Hallier appear there, just to show everyone they are no longer on speaking terms- a show in itself. However, let's go back in time as this is a book of remembrance.

After the Lycée Charlemagne, I went back to the Left Bank to take up intermittent university studies. I went first to the Lycée Louis le Grand, then to the Sorbonne but not for long. At Louis le Grand, my classics master, Goube, was a fanatic of Latin prose, a visionary of Greek abstractions. He had outlived Buchenwald concentration camp, so he said, because he was so absorbed in the joyous preparation of Latin prose for the coming year that he ignored the guards. Goube was modesty and integrity incarnate, fired with the desire to bring dead languages back to life. Much later I found that same passion, that same love of words brought back from the dead. The words were Hebrew and the man was Ben Gurion. At Louis le Grand a small sheep-like man from Alsace, Jacques Ullman, who pulled at his cuffs before pronouncing a decisive sentence, taught philosophy. He summed up Hegel's philosophical ideas with miraculous clarity, incorporating in his lectures doubt and irony, both of which were singularly lacking in the original writings. As an aside, Ullman denounced unassumingly the sectarian and ideological fanaticism which had begun to attract many of us. I firmly declare, even if it shocks, that Ullmans and Goubes, even if they come from Colmar or Poitiers can only blossom forth in Paris.

So be it; although I love Bordeaux, centralization is part of my make-up. In the whole of France nothing can replace the steep slope of the rue Saint Jacques nor the rue des Ecoles — Shame to the name! — which cuts it crisscross. My soul is that of a Parisian — what can I do about it? I cannot imagine Sartre writing *La Nausée (Nausea)* or Ionesco writing *Les Chaises* anywhere but in Paris. One man perceived that spell of zinc and lead and tiles: the film director Marcel Carné. Carné liked to rebuild Paris on location. Go and see *Le jour se lève (Daybreak; 1944)* and *Les Portes de la Nuit (1947)*. He produced what literature could not evoke: Paris, its cruelty, its furtively tender, humourless irony.

My great-grandfather was a local councillor at Pré Saint Gervais. He had been, so I gather, a deputy of Jean Jaurès, the left-wing political leader who was assassinated in 1914. My great-grandfather worked as a cabinet maker. One day he delivered a cabinet to Auteuil — in 1912 so I was told. He came back puffed-out, loosened his tie, asked for a stiff drink and said, "The country is suffocating". I have inherited his typically Parisian mistrust of ploughed fields and greenery unless a river flows or a pond dozes. Parisians, the genuine stock, those who do not lie to themselves, go to the country because they have been told how beautiful and how healthy it is but they never stay long. They cannot do without certain regularly recurring elements in their lives: the Edgar Quinet Market every other day, or the bells of Saint Germain l'Auxerrois on which the composer Renaud Gagneux improvises every Wednesday. The Parisian, even if he was born at Saint-Flour, prefers his germs to the fresh air of the country. The farmers are aware of the fact and generally have little liking for us.

Today I live in a village of steel, looming above the Montparnasse railway station. On the concrete walkway there is sliver of grass that seems almost too lavish. In spring a blackbird sings every morning at 5 a.m. The female flies in, under the lighted street-lamps. It is fabulous. In my village of steel there are all the shades of Braque's paintings, even purple. Everyone knows everyone else and stops to exchange a few words just as they do in Berlin or in Spain. My village is like the Gaullist party in France: everyone has been, is, or will be a member of it.

Its villagers live and intrigue punctiliously. Of course elsewhere, there is the rue de la Solitude, the rue de l'Estrapade, the rue Tournefort and its cryptic stones. But at this angle of the rue du Maine you can still stroll and admire the birds, among which is the kestrel flying home to its nest on Notre-Dame Cathedral. That is my Paris, a cosmopolitan patchwork of Greeks, Chileans and Tamils, timorous people who have suffered under odious regimes; a city peopled by Czechs, Russians and Poles; by old ladies, former friends of long-dead Viennese composers, who take afternoon tea at La Coupole.

That is the dauntless and disrespectful city in which I have written these lines, a stone's throw away from the Select — a city I shall never leave.

GAULOISES
allumettes BLONDES

Rothmans
BRIQUETS

PHILIP MORRIS
100ᵐᵐ

Allumettes
GITANES
BLONDES

20

The storm turned you into sublime poetry.
(A. Rimbaud)

*... One could
see a countless flock
of old roofs...
(V. Hugo)*

Musicians love Paris
so much that they use its river banks
as fabulous opera settings
(C. Semprun Maura)

Pont des arts

What then can love be when dreaming of it is so sweet ?
(A. de Lamartine)

Shivering dawn draped in pink and green
Moved slowly down the empty Seine...
(C. Baudelaire)

Under the pont St-Michel,
as well as under the pont Mirabeau,
"the Seine and our loves flow,
must I remember them ?"
(G. Apollinaire)

Free man,
you will always
cherish the sea !
(C. Baudelaire)

Architecture (and I include practically
all constructed objects
in that word)
must be sensual and material
as well as spiritual
and speculative.
(Le Corbusier)

Paris has become
a monster spread over
a whole region, a monster of
the most elementary biological type :
a protoplasm, a blotch.
(Le Corbusier)

*A victory for children's dreams
and a victory for the funfair,
revelry continues
in the Tuileries gardens.
(C. Semprun Maura)*

*From our lofty thoughts
look down on servile cities
As fatal rocks human
enslavement is tied to.
(A. de Vigny)*

Small showers,
calm high winds.
Long drinking breaks up thunderstorms.
(F. Rabelais)

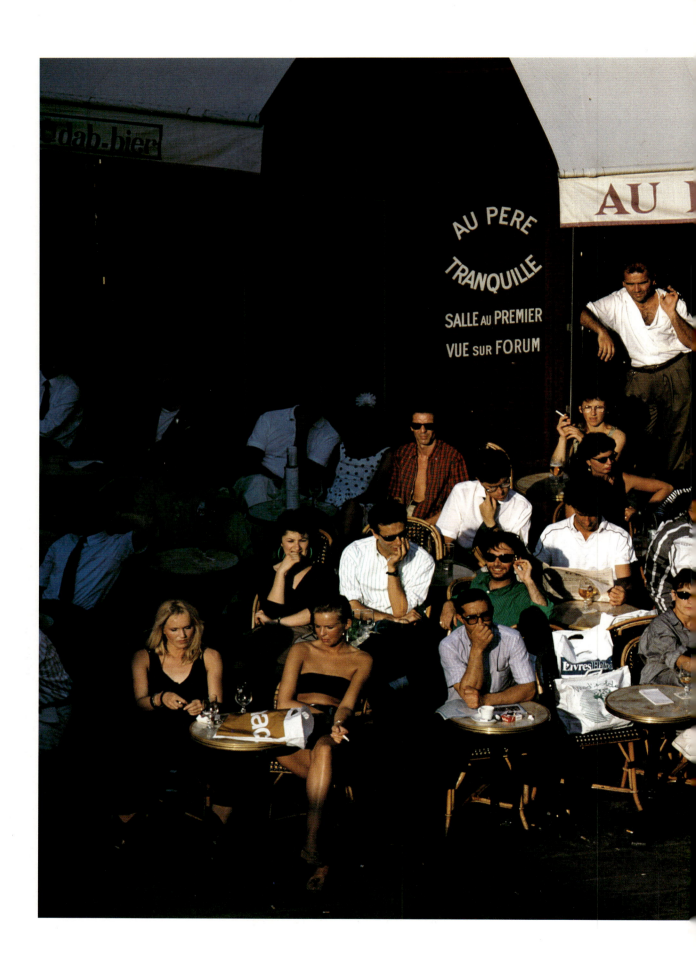

Everywhere, as is said in that story
Everywhere, one may laugh and sing
Everywhere, one may love and drink
Our aim, our aim is liberty !
(R. Clair)

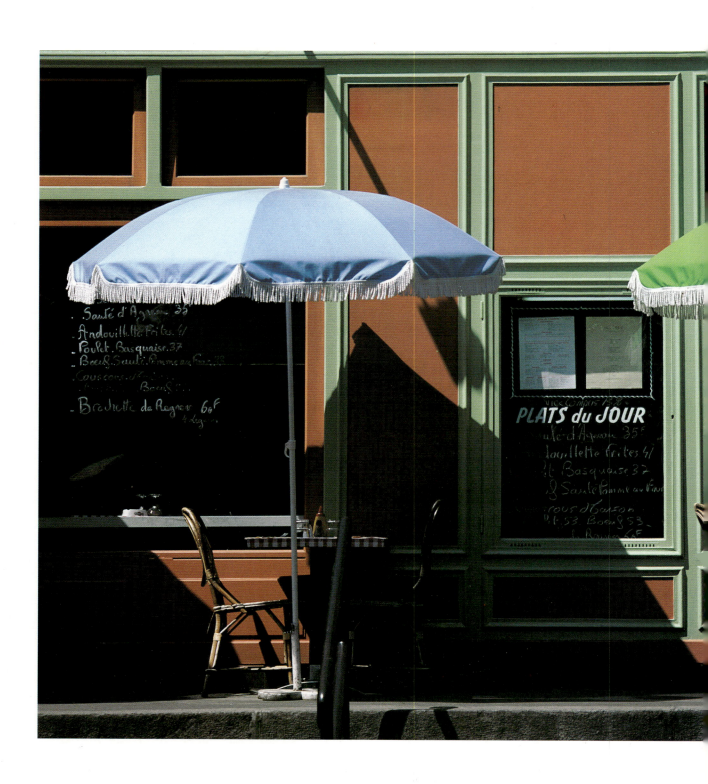

I shall have lived out
my life in pavement cafés.
(C. Semprun Maura)

In a word, the streets of Paris
have human qualities...
(H. de Balzac)

There are clumsy artists, there are no clumsy styles.
(A. Malraux)

Fashion is a tyrant from
whom nothing can deliver us...
(E. Pavillon)

*This display of masculine
erotic fantasies is also,
or mainly, a giggle.
(C. Semprun Maura)*

Anything that is neither a colour
nor a scent nor music
is mere triviality.
(B. Vian)

The little ladies of Paris

From woman comes light and, morning as evening,
life is shaped around her.
(L. Aragon)

In Paris sweetness and love,
wealth and honour
have taken up their abode.
(P. Desportes)

Stone horses go round in the bizarre dreams of heroism.
(C. Semprun Maura)

To fledglings he gives their food,
and his goodness is extended to all creation.
(J. Racine)

All nature's secrets
lie open to the heavens and we see them every day
without paying attention.
(A. Gide)

*The horror of boredom and
the love of quiet :
the supreme art is to avoid
the former without damaging
the latter...
(G. Senac de Meilhan)*

Those who are fed up to the teeth Sunday afternoon because they can see Monday looming, and Tuesday, and Wednesday, and Thursday, and Friday and Saturday, and Sunday afternoon.
(J. Prévert)

When he went to
the Horticultural Gardens
(Jardin des Plantes)
the sight of a palm tree
transported him to
foreign countries.
(G. Flaubert)

Paris is the metropolis
of dissipation,
and it is there
that the idlest by temperament
and situation are the busiest
(C. Pinot Duclos)

The idler and the kid are the alpha and omega of Paris.
(V. Hugo)

To breathe in Paris
conserves the soul.
(V. Hugo)

*Children are bored
on Sundays, Trenet sang,
but who has sung of
the boredom of ponies?
(L. Torres)*

*My soul is wafted
on perfume like
the souls of others
on music.
(C. Baudelaire)*

If looking could wear things out...
(G. Flaubert)

On the Seine

If we do not sleep it is to watch for the dawn
Which will prove that we are at last living the present.
(R. Desnos)

Mirrors would do well
to reflect a little longer
before sending back an image.
(J. Cocteau)

*Architecture is
a way of thinking,
not a job.
(Le Corbusier)*

The minimum that one demands of a sculpture is that it remain motionless.
(S. Dali)

*The most profound thinker
remains such
a clockwork figure.
(D. Diderot)*

The peasants of Paris.
(L. Aragon)

Beaubourg

Fellini's casting.
(F. Barreyre)

Improvised volcanoes

Buskers' fiery throats.
(P. Ganier Raymond)

Paris is a feast.
(E. Hemingway)

The little Saturday night dance...
(J. Drejac)

Listen to my sweet song
That only weeps for your pleasure.
(P. Verlaine)

Let us just say that the Theatre, like Life, is a dream,
without worrying overmuch about its veracity.
(J.L. Barrault)

*My kingdom
for a horse.
(W. Shakespeare)*

Horses, uniforms and
waving feathers :
the parade of the Garde Republicaine
enchants passers-by.
(J. Launay)

Grandeur and traditions
of these servants of the nation.
(J. Launay)

The people want to end it all ;
but there is no end.
(P.J. Proudhon)

The new surrealist age
of "cannibalism of objects"
warrants this conclusion :

... *"Beauty will be eatable*
or will not exist".
(S. Dali)

*Eternally conjugating
the verb "to love"
may only be suitable
for totally artless creatures.
(G. de Nerval)*

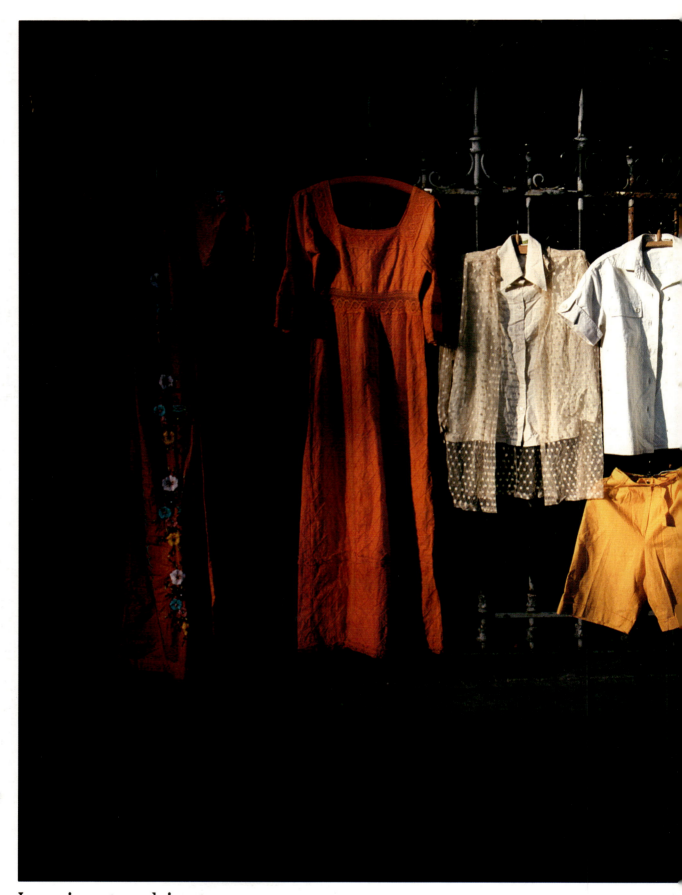

Inanimate objects

... have you a soul...
(A. de Lamartine)

*In this bazaar
new goods are generally
prohibited...
(E. Sue)*

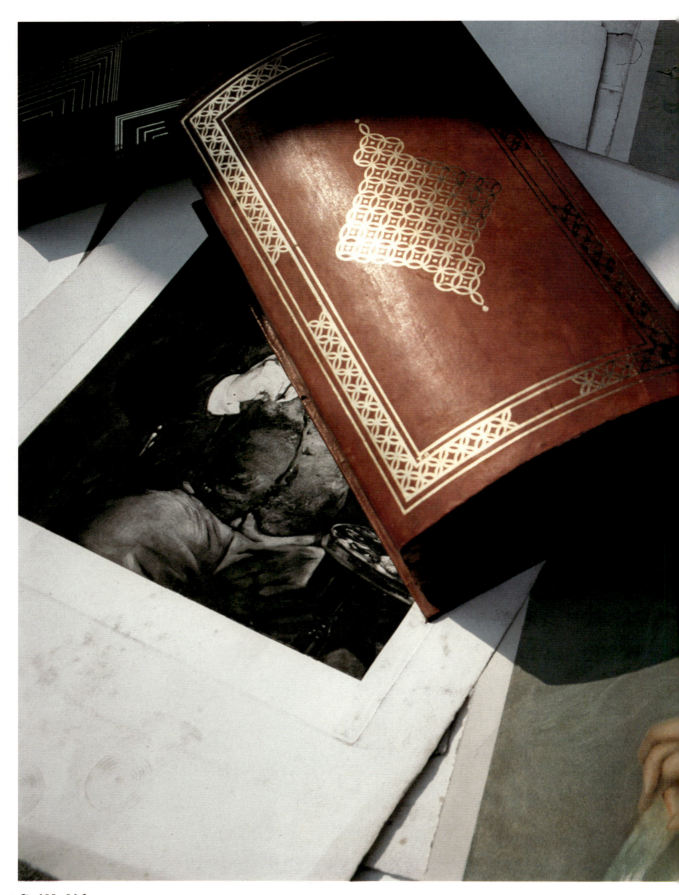

Still life

Which door do you push open into what corridor once you have fallen asleep ?
(J. Cocteau)

The Madame Tussauds (musée Grévin)
of quick-change fashion.
(P. Ganier Raymond)

*All men are secretly
attracted by ruins.
(F.R. de Chateaubriand)*

Farewell Bercy !

Farewell Bercy !
When the house vibrated
like a great stone heart
With all those joyful hearts
beating beneath its roof.
(A. de Lamartine)

Be more in love than ever ;
Rush to paint beautiful women,
And let the reward for your paintings
Be the embraces of your models.
(B. de Bonnard)

Beauty of form...

... purity, unity and
truth hold stricken nature
to the ground.
(G. Apollinaire)